The Arab World Thought of It

The Arab World Thought of It

INVENTIONS, INNOVATIONS, AND AMAZING FACTS

Saima S. Hussain

annick press
toronto + new york + vancouver

© 2013 Saima S. Hussain (text)
Edited by David MacDonald
Maps on pp. 10–11 by Tina Holdcroft

Annick Press Ltd.

We acknowledge the support of the Canada Council for the Arts, the Ontario Arts Council, and the Government of Canada through the Canada Book Fund (CBF) for our publishing activities.

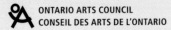 ONTARIO ARTS COUNCIL
CONSEIL DES ARTS DE L'ONTARIO

Cataloging in Publication

Hussain, Saima S.
    The Arab world thought of it : inventions, innovations, and amazing facts / Saima S. Hussain.

(We thought of it)
Includes bibliographical references and index.
Issued also in electronic format.
ISBN 978-1-55451-477-9 (bound).—ISBN 978-1-55451-476-2 (pbk.)

    1. Civilization, Arab—Juvenile literature. I. Title.
II. Series: We thought of it

DS36.8.H88 2013   j909'.0974927   C2012-905788-6

Distributed in Canada by:
Firefly Books Ltd.
66 Leek Crescent
Richmond Hill, ON L4B 1H1

Published in the U.S.A. by Annick Press (U.S.) Ltd.
Distributed in the U.S.A. by:
Firefly Books (U.S.) Inc.
P.O. Box 1338
Ellicott Station
Buffalo, NY 14205

Printed in China

Visit us at: www.annickpress.com

For my family, especially my nephews Ammad and Omar. And for the family of Mohamed Bouazizi, the Tunisian street vendor who, by dying, gave birth to the Arab Spring. May his sacrifice not have been in vain. —S.S.H.

Contents

Marhaba, Welcome.

In my memories of growing up in the Kingdom of Saudi Arabia, I remember the desert, looking much as it must have centuries ago, and the tall palm trees that have always grown in the region. Occasionally I would even see a camel in the desert. My mother and I would sometimes go to a traditional outdoor marketplace, called a *souk*, to buy spices and cloth, just as people did long ago. But I also have memories that show how Saudi Arabia has changed from times past. There were tall office buildings along modern highways, where luxury cars and early versions of today's SUVs were everywhere. We did most of our shopping in grocery stores and malls, which—like homes and office buildings—were air-conditioned to provide relief from the very hot sun. The Saudi Arabia of my childhood was a mix of old and new, and this is true of the Arab world today.

Who is an Arab? A simple answer is to say that an Arab is someone whose first language is Arabic and who can trace his or her family's history to the Middle East or North Africa. (Not

The Liberation Tower in Kuwait City, Kuwait

everyone would agree with this definition. For example, there are members of some groups, such as Coptic Egyptians and North African Berbers, who fit the definition but do not consider themselves Arabs.) While most Arabs are Muslims, there are also many Arab Christians, as well as Arab Jews.

Arabs have a very long and fascinating history. When I lived in Saudi Arabia, I learned some of this history at school and some from my parents and grandparents, who told me about important people and events from the past. Later, when I studied history at the University of Toronto, I learned a lot more.

One of the things I learned was that many centuries ago all Arabs lived in the area called the Arabian Peninsula, once known as Arabia (see page 10). Most of Arabia was desert, with some fertile areas where grains, coffee, and fruits were grown.

The Great Mosque in Cordoba, Spain, is now a UNESCO World Heritage Site.

Some Arabs were Bedouins—desert nomads who moved from place to place and invented useful things such as tents. Bedouin Arabs did not own land or houses. They considered their camels, horses, and sheep to be their wealth.

Other Arabs lived in fertile areas and developed better farming techniques to make the best use of the little land where crops could grow. There were also Arabs who made their living as traders, traveling around the world by land and sea, buying luxury goods to sell to buyers in Europe. From India and China, Arab traders bought goods such as spices, silk, and jewels. From Africa they bought gold, which they traded for salt.

Around the year 629 CE, groups of young Arab men set out to conquer other parts of the world and create a large empire. Many of them married and lived in the places they conquered—including Spain, where Arabs ruled for 700 years. Over time, Arab language and culture and the Muslim religion spread all over this empire, and even outside of it.

Arabs who lived in this empire built schools, hospitals, and beautiful palaces. They were responsible for the translation of many Latin and Greek books into Arabic so that more people could learn from them. They also carried out research in chemistry, physics, astronomy, agriculture, medicine, math, and geography, among other subjects.

Today, most Arabs live in the 22 countries that make up the League of Arab States (see page 10). There are also many people living in other parts of the world who can trace their roots to an Arab country. Well-known examples include the singer Shakira, who was born in Colombia but is proud of her Arab background (her name is Arabic for "thankful"); North American celebrities Salma Hayek, Paula Abdul, and Tony Shalhoub; and two Arab Americans who won the Nobel Prize for Chemistry, Dr. Ahmed H. Zewail and Dr. Elias Corey.

Let's get going on our journey into the Arab world. On this journey we will meet some Arabs who became famous for their inventions and innovations over the centuries.

A coral reef off the coast of Egypt

THE ARAB WORLD TODAY

The countries labeled on the map below are today considered to be part of the Arab world. All of these countries belong to a group called the League of Arab States. Long ago, the area shown in darker brown was known as Arabia. Today, people sometimes call this area the Arabian Peninsula.

THE ARAB EMPIRE IN 750 CE

In ancient times, the Arab empire grew as Arabs conquered neighboring lands. Around 750 CE, the empire was at its largest and included the areas shown in brown below.

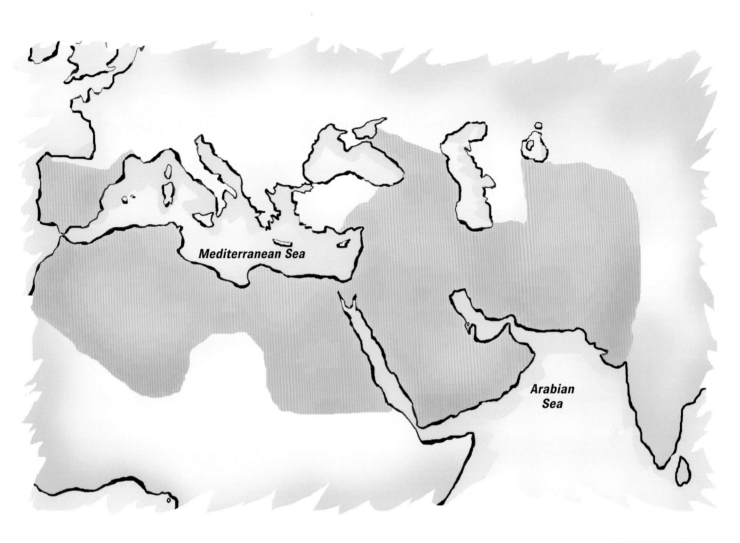

Mediterranean Sea

Arabian Sea

The Hoggar Mountains in Algeria

Rocky coastline in Qatar

TIMELINE

Long ago, in a period stretching back to at least 900 BCE, the land known as Arabia (see page 10) was divided into many small kingdoms and tribes, which were each ruled by a king or tribal chief. In 622 CE, the Prophet Muhammad (see page 28) began to unite these kingdoms and tribes into what became an Arab empire. The empire grew over time, eventually including regions as far west as Spain and as far east as parts of India.

The Arab empire was ruled by a caliph (similar to a king, but a caliph was also a religious leader). When a caliph died, he was usually replaced by a younger member of his family. A series of rulers from the same family was

First built during the Umayyad caliphate, the Mosque of Uqba (also known as the Great Mosque of Kairouan) in Tunisia was later expanded during the Abbasid caliphate. Above: The interior of the Mosque of Uqba

900 BCE–622 CE
Many Arabian kingdoms and tribes

622–632
Muhammad begins to create a united Arab empire

632–661
Rashidun caliphate

661–750
Umayyad caliphate

750–1258
Abbasid caliphate

A ceramic dish made in Syria during the Fatimid Caliphate

called a "caliphate." Each caliphate was given a name (see the timeline below), often based on the name of the first ruler.

As the empire grew very large, the original empire founded by Arabs became multicultural. Many of the people living in this empire were not Arabs, but the Arabic language was used in areas such as government, law, and the study of religion. During the time of the Fatimid caliphate and the Seljuk empire, the caliph from the Abbasid caliphate was still the over-all ruler of the empire.

In 1299 CE, a Turkish soldier named Othman al-Ghazi founded the Ottoman empire. When an Ottoman army defeated the Mamluks in 1517, the Ottomans became rulers of the Arab world. They made Constantinople (now called Istanbul, which is in modern-day Turkey) their capital city.

A modern-day view of Istanbul, Turkey

1250–1517
Mamluk empire

1517–1919
Ottoman caliphate

1919–1971
European colonial rule in some areas

1932–present
Independent Arab countries

909–1171
Fatimid caliphate

1037–1194
Seljuk empire

A battle ax with decorative engraving made during the Ottoman Caliphate

PLACES OF LEARNING

Long ago in the Arab world, most learning took place in mosques (buildings where Muslims worship), which also served as community centers. Men went to mosques every day to pray and to exchange thoughts and opinions. But there were also other places where people learned new things.

An old, handwritten Arab book about astronomy

Public Libraries

Ancient Egyptians, Greeks, and Romans all built libraries. Only rich people and scholars were allowed to use these libraries, and no one was allowed to borrow books to read at home. Arabs were the first to build public libraries where anyone could enter and borrow books, if they agreed to take good care them.

Mosques in almost every big city of the Arab empire contained a library. The librarians who ran the libraries were highly respected because they were considered to be the protectors of knowledge.

The largest and earliest Arab public library was probably the Sayfiya, which was started around 960 CE and was located inside the Great Umayyad Mosque in Aleppo, Syria. The al-Aqsa Mosque in the city of Jerusalem had four libraries. (The Arabic name for Jerusalem is al-Quds.) In 1258 CE the city of Baghdad (now the capital city of Iraq) was home to 36 public libraries.

Scholars at work in the House of Wisdom

The House of Wisdom

One caliph, named al-Mamun (pronounced *al-mamoon*), was especially fond of learning. In about 802 CE, he built a great learning center in the city of Baghdad and called it the House of Wisdom. Many famous scientists and doctors from across the Arab empire came to the House of Wisdom to share information.

Al-Mamun also sent translators to other parts of the world so they could read books, translate them into Arabic, and send the translations to the library at the House of Wisdom. In this way, many important books were translated into Arabic for the first time. Because al-Mamun made such an important contribution to learning in the ancient Arab world, some historians call him the "master of Arab civilization."

A modern library in Egypt

Free Schools

In the ancient civilizations of Greece and Rome, schools were not free and only rich families could afford the high cost. The first free school for children in the Arab world began in 653 CE in a mosque in the city of Medina (sometimes spelled Madina), which is now part of Saudi Arabia. Along with subjects such as religion, math, and poetry, students learned how to care for animals and plants.

Advanced Learning

Over time, some of the free schools became places for advanced learning where people from all over the Arab world—and even from outside it—came to study subjects such as law, engineering, religion, and history. In many ways, these schools were similar to modern colleges and universities—there were dorms where students could live, cafeterias, and libraries.

Some of these schools still exist and have now become modern universities. A school that was started in 972 CE eventually became al-Azhar University in Cairo, Egypt. The school that became the University of al-Qarawiyin in Fez, Morocco, was founded in 859 CE. According to many experts, this is the oldest university still operating today.

A building designed to look like a book at the King Fahd University of Petroleum and Minerals in Saudi Arabia

The University of al-Qarawiyin in Morocco

ASTRONOMY AND FLIGHT

Arabs made important contributions to many areas of science. One was astronomy (the study of stars and planets). A historic "first" in the history of flight took place in the Arab world.

Observatories

An observatory is a building with equipment that allows astronomers to study stars and planets. Observatories are often built at high altitudes and away from city lights so astronomers can get a clear view of the night sky.

Around the 9th century CE, the caliph al-Mamun was very interested in helping scholars—including astronomers—learn new things. He decided to have an observatory built in Shamasiyah, on the outskirts of Baghdad. It was completed in 828 CE, and some experts believe it was the first observatory ever constructed. In 830 CE, al-Mamun ordered another observatory to be built at Mount Qasiyun in Damascus (now the capital city of Syria). Because it was built on a mountain, this observatory offered a better view of stars and planets and was used to confirm what astronomers had observed at the Shamasiyah observatory.

Arabs were not the first to study the sun, moon, stars, and planets, but they were the first to do it from observatories with large instruments, as part of an organized scientific project involving several astronomers. By observing the night sky, astronomers learned how to predict the movement of planets and the phases of the moon.

A 16th-century painting of astronomers at work

Arabic Star Names

The original names for many stars were Arabic because these stars were studied or discovered by Arab astronomers. Some of these stars are now known by different names, which are based on the original Arabic names. For example, the current names of stars in the constellation (or group of stars) that we call the Big Dipper come from the original Arabic names.

On this diagram of the Big Dipper, the original Arabic star names are in green, and the names currently used are in white.

Dub
Dubhe

Maraqq
Merak

Maghraz
Megrez

al-Hawar
Alioth

Fakhdha
Phecda

Mi'zar
Mizar

al-Qa'id
Alkaid

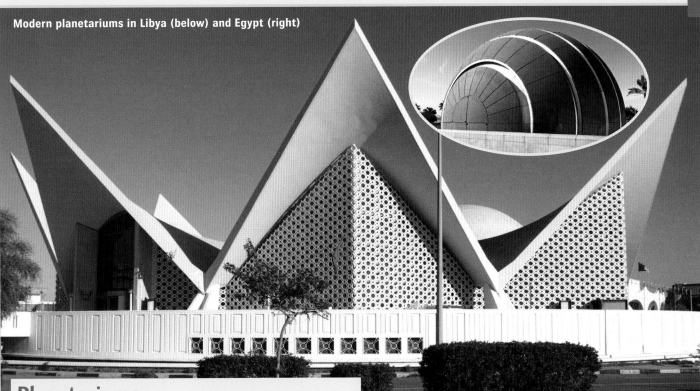

Modern planetariums in Libya (below) and Egypt (right)

Planetariums

A modern planetarium is a large room or theater where the stars, planets, and other natural objects visible in the night sky are projected onto the ceiling. The effect is so real that audiences could almost believe that they are actually looking at the night sky, or even sitting in outer space.

According to a historian writing around 1600 CE, in the 9th century CE an engineer named Abbas ibn Firnas created a room in his house where spectators could view stars and clouds, and were astounded by thunder and lightning. These effects were all created by machinery hidden in the basement. This was the world's first planetarium, and it even had sound effects!

First Attempt at Flight

Abbas ibn Firnas is even better known for his flying machine. There are many ancient legends about humans trying to fly, but the first recorded attempt to build and use a flying machine was made by Ibn Firnas in 852 CE. He created a contraption out of wood and silk and tried to fly it off the roof of the Grand Mosque in Cordoba, Spain. Almost immediately, he came crashing down.

Ibn Firnas made improvements to his design and added eagle feathers. For his second attempt, he took off from a hill outside Cordoba. To the amazement of the crowd below, he flew for at least 10 minutes. Ibn Firnas was 70 years old at the time of his successful flight. Today, an airport in Baghdad is named after him.

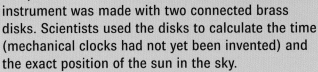

An astrolabe made in Syria during the 16th century

Universal Astrolabe

Think of an astrolabe as a type of ancient computer. This complicated instrument was made with two connected brass disks. Scientists used the disks to calculate the time (mechanical clocks had not yet been invented) and the exact position of the sun in the sky.

Most astrolabes were designed to be used at a particular location, so they did not give accurate information when used at other locations. That problem was solved in the 11th century CE, when two Arab scientists named al-Shakkaz and al-Zarqali developed the universal astrolabe. Because this device gave accurate information anywhere it was used, it was very helpful for travelers who wanted to know the correct time at various places on their journey.

MEDICINE

Arabs contributed a great deal to research and innovation in the field of medicine. Most famous of all is the physician Qasim al-Zahrawi, who is sometimes called "the father of modern surgery" because many of his ideas are still used today by surgeons around the world.

A modern scalpel

Surgical Instruments

Qasim al-Zahrawi was born in Cordoba, Spain, in 936 CE. He invented over 100 surgical instruments, including the scalpel (a surgical knife), the surgical needle (used to close wounds with stitches), and surgical scissors. These types of surgical instruments are still used by surgeons today.

Many of the surgical instruments al-Zahrawi invented were illustrated and discussed for the first time in his book titled *On Surgery*. This is one in a series of 30 books he wrote, which together form an encyclopedia, *The Method of Medicine*, that was published around 1000 CE. For over 500 years after it was published, medical students in universities all over Europe studied al-Zahrawi's medical encyclopedia.

A modern curved surgical needle used for stitches

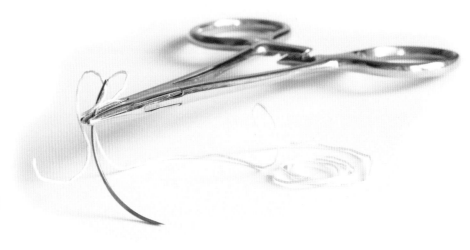

Pharmacies

Pharmacies, or drugstores, existed in the Arab world in ancient times, as early as 754 CE or perhaps even earlier. Pharmacists created ointments, pills, powders, and syrups that were used as medicines to treat illnesses. In later times, pharmacies were visited by government inspectors, who checked the quality of the medicines that were made. The inspectors also made sure that pharmacies were not selling medicines that had been shown to be ineffective.

A Jordanian pharmacist

Catgut for Internal Stitches

As a surgeon, al-Zahrawi often needed to stitch up cuts he had made inside a patient's body. Regular thread was not safe to use inside the body, but he discovered something that was.

The story goes that al-Zahrawi's cat swallowed the strings of an oud (a type of guitar), and he worried that the cat might become ill. Once he was sure that his cat had suffered no harm, he wanted to find out why. Al-Zahrawi discovered that oud strings were made out of catgut (a natural material that comes from animals such as sheep or goats—but not cats). He realized that catgut could safely be used to stitch up his patients.

We don't know for certain whether the story about the cat is true, but we do know that al-Zahrawi encouraged other doctors to use surgical thread made from catgut. One of the benefits of stitches made from catgut is that they dissolve on their own over time, so they do not need to be removed. Catgut surgical thread is still used for stitches today.

Modern surgeons still sometimes use thread made from catgut for stitches.

Today, doctors and nurses use cotton balls soaked with alcohol to kill germs on the skin before giving an injection.

Treating Wounds

Al-Zahrawi was likely the first doctor in the Arab world to use purified alcohol as an antiseptic to clean wounds. He realized that deep wounds can become infected if they are not properly cleaned. He was also the first to use pieces of cotton to cover cuts and control bleeding.

Cataract Surgery

A cataract is cloudy material that develops in the eye, making it difficult to see clearly. This condition is common among senior citizens, and thanks to a man named Ammar al-Mawsili, it can be corrected with simple surgery.

Al-Mawsili was born in Iraq but worked as a surgeon in Egypt. Around 1000 CE, he invented a special syringe and a hollow needle that he used to suck the cataract out of the eye, allowing his patients to see clearly again. The surgical instruments and the procedure used in modern cataract surgery are very similar to those invented by al-Mawsili.

Modern cataract surgery

ARTS AND CRAFTS

People of all cultures like to make and look at beautiful things, and this is certainly true of Arabs. Among the beautiful things created in the Arab world are stained glass windows, decorative calligraphy, and arabesque designs.

Pottery

In the 8th and 9th centuries CE, Arabs came up with some important innovations related to pottery (objects made of baked clay). One of these was decorating porcelain with blue designs on a white background. Many people are familiar with this style of decoration on Chinese pottery, but experts claim that Arabs were the first to use it.

Glaze is a special kind of paint used to put color on the surface of pottery. Arabs discovered a way to improve glaze so that pottery could hold liquids without the liquids seeping into the clay. In Iraq, craftsmen developed "luster glaze," which had such a brilliant shine that it made pottery look as if it were made of a polished metal such as gold or silver.

A vase made in Syria during the 14th century

Stained glass windows from an old mosque in Egypt

Stained Glass Windows

Some European churches that were built as early as the 4th century CE seem to have stained glass windows, but these windows are not really glass. They are made of thin, colored slices of alabaster, a mineral that allows light to shine through it.

The mosque known as Dome of the Rock (called *Kubbet es-Sukhrah* in Arabic) was one of the first buildings with real stained glass windows. Built in Jerusalem in 691 CE, this mosque had 16 stained glass windows, which were decorated with verses from the Quran. (For more information on the Quran, see page 29.)

Arabic Calligraphy

Arabs are proud of the Arabic language and take pride in writing it as beautifully as possible. The art of decorative writing is called "calligraphy" and, around the 8th century CE, Arabs developed unique styles of calligraphy for writing verses from the Quran.

To make ink of many different colors, Arabs used natural materials such as tea, onion skins, bark from the pomegranate tree, and other plants. Sometimes even fragrance was added to the ink so the calligraphy would have a pleasant smell. Like modern calligraphers, Arab calligraphers of the past used pen nibs made from the stalk of the reed plant. Nibs made of reed are more flexible than metal nibs, so they make it easier to create the curves and circles found in Arabic writing. (For more information on Arabic writing, see page 42.)

Beautiful examples of Arabic calligraphy are found not only in books but also on the walls of buildings such as mosques and palaces, both old and modern.

Arabic calligraphy carved into a palace wall

Arabesque

Arab artists are famous for a style of decoration known as arabesque—elaborate geometrical designs filled with many tiny details. When you look very closely at these designs, you can see that they are made of lines, circles, and patterns repeated many times to create an interesting effect. Arabesque is used to decorate the ceilings and walls of buildings, as well as fabrics, carpets, furniture, and other household objects.

Arabesque designs on an Egyptian lamp from the 14th century

WEAPONS AND WAR

Long ago, Arabs conquered many new lands to expand their empire (see the map on page 11). Winning a war requires good weapons and effective ways of fighting a battle. Arabs had some interesting "firsts" in both of these areas.

Recipes for Gunpowder

The Chinese invented gunpowder, which they used in fireworks, but it is not clear whether Chinese or Arab inventors were the first to figure out how to use gunpowder in weapons of war. Evidence suggests that both groups had discovered how to do this by early in the 10th century CE. However, we do know that Arabs went on to develop many unique recipes for gunpowder.

Around 1295 CE, a Syrian scholar named Hasan al-Rammah wrote *The Book of Military Horsemanship and Ingenious War Devices*. This book contained 107 recipes for making gunpowder, which al-Rammah said had been passed down from his father and grandfather. Gunpowder made from these recipes helped Arabs to win many battles.

Some early forms of gunpowder were made with the ingredients shown above (from left to right): potassium nitrate, sulfur, and powdered charcoal.

Torpedo

In *The Book of Military Horsemanship and Ingenious War Devices*, Hasan al-Rammah described a weapon called the "egg," which he said "moves itself and burns." With the help of illustrations and detailed descriptions, al-Rammah explained how this device could be built and filled with gunpowder. It would then be launched from one of the large sailing ships used in battle, and would travel on the water's surface to attack and destroy an enemy ship. This weapon was the world's first torpedo.

Today, torpedoes are still used in warfare, and they are often launched from submarines.

A torpedo being launched from a modern warship

Midfa

In 1249 CE, Arab soldiers used a new weapon called a midfa to fight off the invading French army. The *midfa* was a wooden bowl filled with gunpowder and covered with a large stone. When the gunpowder was lit, it exploded and the stone flew with great force toward the enemy. This weapon was an early form of what later became known as a cannon.

The midfa was an early form of the type of cannon shown here. Both weapons used gunpowder to create an explosion that launched a missile.

Camels in War

Camels have been used in desert wars throughout history. In 853 BCE, an Arab king named Gindibu contributed 1,000 camels to an army he joined to fight against a neighboring empire. As far as historians know, this was the first time camels were used in a desert war.

Camels were considered very useful in desert warfare because they can survive for a long time with little or no water. There was also another benefit to using camels—horses often panic when they smell camels. When an enemy's horses smelled the camels, the horses might refuse to obey the commands of the soldiers riding them.

Today, Egypt, Morocco, and Jordan use camels for patrolling desert areas.

Police officers patrolling on camels in Jordan

Arabian Horses

About 4,500 years ago, Bedouin Arabs in the Arabian Peninsula created a new breed of horse called the Arabian horse, which they used to fight wars. The Arabian horse is a special breed of riding horse known for its speed, intelligence, and beauty. Arabian horses are also very comfortable with people, so they are easy to control.

Bedouins were once nomads who lived in tents as they traveled across the desert. An especially good Arabian horse might be given space inside a Bedouin family's tent to protect it from sandstorms and very cold desert nights, as well as thieves.

From the Arabian Peninsula, Arabian horses spread throughout the world. Many famous historical figures (including Napoleon Bonaparte and George Washington) rode Arabian horses. Today, Arabians are still a very popular breed around the world and are used for pleasure riding and competitive events.

FOOD

Sharing food with family, friends, and visitors is a very important part of Arab culture. Many traditional Arab foods and dishes are now popular all over the world.

Three-Course Meals

In the 9th century CE, there lived a man known as Ziryab (which means "blackbird") because of his amazing singing voice. Ziryab started new trends in both fashion and food. Born in Iraq, Ziryab later moved to Cordoba, Spain, where he was hired by the caliph. The caliph wanted Ziryab to teach people in his court how to live a more elegant lifestyle. Ziryab introduced the idea of three-course meals. He said that meals should start with a soup, be followed by a main course of fish or meat, and end with something sweet for dessert. Three-course meals are still popular in homes and restaurants around the world.

Drinking Coffee

Coffee beans were first discovered in the African country of Ethiopia, but Arabs were the first people to make the drink we know as coffee (called *qahwa* in Arabic). Coffee beans were roasted and ground into a powder, which was then boiled in water.

Coffee contains a chemical called "caffeine" that helps people stay awake and alert. Religious men living in Yemen began drinking coffee—with sugar added—so they could stay awake and pray all night. Soon, drinking coffee became very popular in the Arab world. Coffee was sold on the streets and in "coffee houses," where people would come to sit and drink coffee with friends.

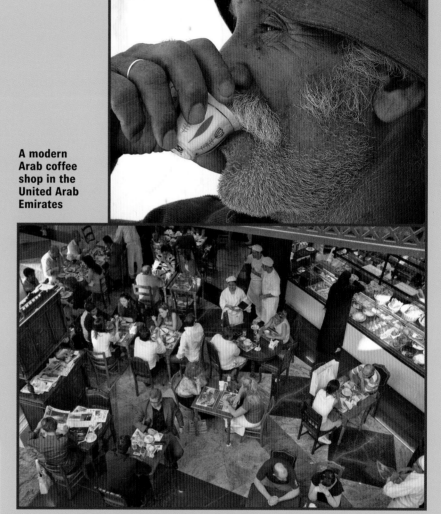

A modern Arab coffee shop in the United Arab Emirates

Tabbouleh

Take some finely chopped tomatoes, cucumber, and green onions. Add boiled bulgur (dried cracked wheat), mint, and lots of chopped parsley. For seasoning, add olive oil, lemon juice, and salt. You have just made tabbouleh, the most popular Arab salad and a dish that is enjoyed around the world. Arabs in the mountains of Syria and Lebanon were the first people to make this delicious salad. If you want to eat tabbouleh in the traditional way, scoop it up with small leaves of lettuce.

Hummus

Hummus is made with mashed chickpeas and sesame seeds, lemon juice, and garlic. This tasty food, which has been popular among Arabs for many hundreds of years, gets its name from its main ingredient—*hummus* is the Arabic word for chickpeas.

Today, although hummus is available in stores in countries around the world, many people still make their own. Some people adapt the traditional recipe by adding olive oil, while others like to make spicy hummus by adding ingredients such as hot jalapeño peppers.

Pita

This round flatbread was first made many hundreds of years ago in Damascus, Syria. Arabs eat it at almost every meal. Pita is so light and thin that when baked in the oven it puffs up in the middle. Cutting off one end of the pita creates a pouch that can be filled with hummus, tabbouleh, and grilled meat to make a sandwich called *shawarma*. Pieces of pita are also often used to scoop up other foods, such as hummus.

Chickpeas

Chickpeas first grew more than 7,000 years ago in what is today part of the Arab world. The earliest chickpea plant was found in the city of Ariha (also called Jericho) near the Jordan River. From there it spread to India and Ethiopia, and was also grown by the ancient Egyptians, Greeks, and Romans. Chickpeas are still a popular food around the world and are valued as a good source of protein and minerals.

Chickpeas growing in pods (above); boiled chickpeas

FOOD *continued*

Sfiha

This traditional food can best be described as "Arab pizza." A small piece of dough is rolled flat and topped with finely chopped meat, pieces of tomato, and oil before it is baked. Sfiha is especially popular in Syria, Jordan, Lebanon, Iraq, and the Palestinian Territories. In the old days, not every house had an oven. Each morning, women would gather at the community brick oven to bake sfiha and bread for their families to eat.

Yogurt

Yogurt made from cow's milk or camel's milk is a popular food in Saudi Arabia and other Arab countries, but strained yogurt has been popular in Arab culture since ancient times. Strained yogurt is firmer than regular yogurt because much of the liquid has been removed.

Long ago, Arabs were nomads who lived in the desert, and they stored camel's milk in bags made of goatskin. The desert heat made liquid evaporate from the milk, turning it into the firm yogurt known as *labneh*. Because it is low in fat and high in protein, labneh is a healthy and nutritious food.

Strained yogurt prepared as a dip

Sherbet

Sherbet

Sherbet is usually made by boiling fresh fruit juice with sugar to create a syrup that is stored in a bottle. Then, whenever a refreshing drink is needed, a little bit of the syrup is mixed with cold water or ice. Some Arabs believe sherbet helps to cool the body in hot weather.

Arabs especially love sherbet made with lemons, oranges, or pomegranates. Many experts believe that the frozen treat we know as sorbet (pronounced *sor-bay*) was developed from sherbet.

Sorbet

Mass Production of Sugar

There is an old saying that goes like this: "Wherever Arabs went, sugar followed." While Indians and Persians were the first people to use sugar, Arabs were the first to produce it in huge quantities. They introduced it to the rest of the world. In many of the lands they conquered, Arabs set up sugar plantations for growing sugarcane (the plant sugar is made from) and sugar factories for making sugar from the sugarcane.

A view of the inside of a stalk of sugarcane

Halwa

Halwa (an Arabic word meaning "sweet") is the name of what is probably the favorite sweet treat in the Arab world. Similar to fudge, halwa can be soft and chewy or a little bit hard. Along with the main ingredients—tahini (sesame seed paste) and sugar—halwa contains various nuts and seeds, such as almonds, pistachios, peanuts, and sunflower seeds. In stores, you may see the name of this delicious food spelled several different ways, such as halva, halvah, and haleweh.

Dates

Many experts believe that dates first grew in eastern Arabia as long ago as 6000 BCE. Different types of dates are grown all over the Arab world. They can be hard or soft, and their color can be black, brown, golden, or red.

For thousands of years, dates have been an important part of the Arab diet. Ancient Arabs carried dates on long journeys across the desert. Why? Dates were a good source of energy for these travelers, and were still tasty once they dried out in the desert heat. Today, people eat dates as a sweet and healthy snack, or add them to desserts and stews.

A fresh date (above) and a dried date (below)

RELIGION

The religion of Islam began in Arabia with a man known as the Prophet Muhammad. People who practice this religion are called Muslims. The Islamic religion is an important part of Arab culture, though not all Muslims are of Arabic heritage and not all Arabs are Muslims.

Crowds of Muslims circle around the Kaaba during the Hajj.

The Kaaba is covered by a black silk cloth embroidered with silver and gold thread. This covering is known as the Kiswa.

The interior of Masjid al-Nabawi (also known as the Mosque of the Prophet) in Medina, where Muhammad is buried

Medina

Muhammad first lived in Mecca. The people of ancient Mecca did not treat Muhammad well, so he fled with a small group of his followers to the nearby city of Yathrib. The people of Yathrib welcomed Muhammad and showed their respect for him by changing the name of their city to Madinat al-Nabi (Arabic for "the City of the Prophet"). Today, most people call the city Medina or Madina.

Medina became the first capital city of the Arab empire, and the first three mosques were built there. Muhammad died in Medina, and his burial place is inside one of the mosques.

Mecca

The city of Mecca is located in what is today Saudi Arabia. In Mecca there is a building called the Kaaba, which is very holy to Muslims. When Muslims around the world pray, they always face the direction that points toward Mecca.

When Muslims visit the Kaaba, they walk around it seven times in a counterclockwise direction. This ritual, called Tawaaf, has a special meaning—by walking together in the same direction, Muslims show that they are united by their religion.

Hajj

Muslims are expected to travel to Mecca at least once in their lifetime, if possible. This visit is known as the Hajj. Every year, Muslims gather in Mecca between the eighth and tenth day of Dhul Hajj (the twelfth and last month of the Islamic calendar) to perform rituals such as Tawaaf. As many as 2 or 3 million people perform the Hajj each year.

The Quran

The Quran (sometimes spelled Koran) is the holy book of Islam. Like the holy books of many religions, the Quran teaches values such as showing kindness to others. Muslims treat their copy of the Quran with great respect, and wash their hands before touching it.

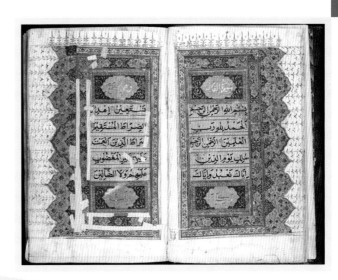

Decorated pages in a Quran over 400 years old

ISLAMIC CELEBRATIONS

Arab Muslims celebrating Ramadan

Ramadan

Ramadan is the ninth month of the Islamic calendar. During this month, Muslims are expected to fast from sunrise until sunset—they avoid eating or drinking anything (even water) until after sunset. Young children, seniors, pregnant women, and those who are sick are not expected to fast. Ramadan is a joyful time for Muslims, and they often decorate mosques with lights. In the Arab world, shops and markets stay open all night, and food is donated to the poor.

Eid al-Fitr

Ramadan ends with the three-day celebration of Eid al-Fitr (pronounced *eed al-fitter*), which is also known as the Feast after the Fast. On the morning of the first day of Eid, people wear their best clothes and go to the mosque for special Eid prayers. After returning home, families sit down to eat a special breakfast together. After breakfast and over the next two days, Muslims continue celebrating by visiting their Muslim neighbors and friends.

Eid al-Adha

The end of the Hajj is celebrated in Mecca and other parts of the world with Eid al-Adha (pronounced *eed al-ad-ha*), also known as the Feast of the Sacrifice. A member of each family sacrifices a goat or sheep, and the meat is divided into three parts: one part is for the family to eat, another part is divided among friends and neighbors, and the third part is donated to the poor.

Many Muslims in North America cannot easily obtain a goat to sacrifice. They may arrange for a relative in another country to make the sacrifice for them, or they may visit special farms where goats are available to Muslims so they can perform this religious sacrifice.

In some countries, Muslim women celebrate Eid al-Fitr by painting their hands with a paste called "henna." The greeting Eid Mubarak ("blessed festival") is used during Eid al-Fitr and Eid al-Adha.

EVERYDAY INVENTIONS

Many objects that we use every day—from pens and mattresses to bars of soap—were invented or improved by Arabs who lived long ago.

Carpets

There are experts who believe that Arab Bedouins living around 7000 BCE were the first people to weave carpets. They spun yarn from the hair of goats and camels or from sheep's wool. The yarn was colored with natural dyes and woven into carpets of different sizes to cover the ground inside their tents. It was a tradition that only women did the weaving. Bedouin carpets were unique because they had designs on both sides.

Tents

It is difficult to determine exactly who first made tents, but experts agree that Bedouin Arabs were among the first, thousands of years ago. Since they moved from place to place, Bedouins needed a portable shelter they could use while crossing the desert. The thick carpets they wove (see above) were ideal for making tents that provided protection from the hot sun and the cold night winds.

Tents made from carpets at a Bedouin camp in the Sahara Desert, Morocco

Pens Containing Ink

The first pens did not contain ink—people had to dip them in ink frequently while writing. These pens were messy and left ink stains on people's hands and clothes. In 953 CE the caliph of Egypt, al-Muizz, ordered inventors to create a pen that contained ink, would not stain his hands or clothes, and would not leak when turned upside down. A few days later, he was presented with a gold pen—the world's first pen that contained ink.

Some modern pens allow people to see how much ink is left inside.

Automatic Clock

The first clocks were sundials created by the ancient Egyptians. Later, water clocks were invented in ancient India and China. These clocks indicated the time through a series of bowls that slowly filled with water, and they had to be watched over by a timekeeper.

In the 13th century CE, an Arab named Ismail al-Jazari made the first automatic clock. It was a water clock but could run on its own, without needing a timekeeper to reset it. For many years, Al-Jazari's clock remained the most accurate machine for telling time.

A modern sundial

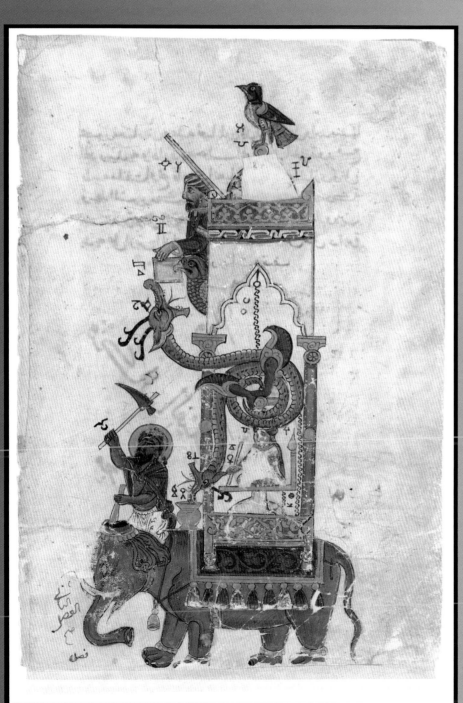

A 14th-century illustration of al-Jazari's Elephant Clock

The Elephant Clock

Probably the most famous of Ismail al-Jazari's many inventions was the Elephant Clock, which stood almost 2 m (6 ft) tall. This water clock symbolized the cultural diversity of the medieval world—it included an Indian elephant ridden by two Arabs using a Persian carpet for a saddle, along with a Chinese dragon and an Egyptian phoenix (a mythical bird). At the very top of the clock was a semicircle that kept track of how many hours of the day had passed.

The Elephant Clock had mechanisms that made many things happen. After every half hour the bowl in the elephant's stomach would fill with water and sink to the bottom. The sinking bowl pulled a rope connected to the phoenix, making it sing and turn around and around. The Arabian figure seated on the top then released one of the two falcons by his side, which in turn released a ball, which the dragon then placed in the vase near the elephant's head, causing the Arabian rider to wave his arms.

EVERYDAY INVENTIONS *continued*

Soap Bars

The ancient Greeks, Romans, and Babylonians all used some form of soap. It was usually made by mixing boiled animal fat and wood ashes with other ingredients to create a liquid soap. The solid soap bars we use today were invented by Arabs. They added scented oils and perfumes to soap to give it a pleasant smell.

In the 13th century CE, soapmaking was a thriving industry in the Arab world. The cities of Aleppo and Damascus (in Syria) and Nablus (in the present-day Palestinian Territories) were famous for making soap bars of very high quality.

Bars of Aleppo soap, which is traditionally made in Aleppo, Syria

New Perfumes

Perfumes have been used since ancient times. In the 9th century CE, a famous mathematician and chemist named Abu Yusuf al-Kindi, born in Kufa, Iraq, wrote *The Book of the Chemistry of Perfume and Distillations*, which contained over 100 new perfume recipes using fruits, plants, and flowers. The book introduced 107 different methods for making perfume, and described new equipment for making perfumes, body sprays, and scented creams.

Perfume bottles from Morocco

Arabic Numerals

Numbers were invented by mathematicians in ancient India, but it was Arabs who developed the shapes of the numbers we use today, called Arabic numerals. Arabic numerals were first seen in print in the 9th century CE, in the works of al-Kindi (see New Perfumes above) and another mathematician, Muhammad al-Khwarizmi. It was not until the 13th century CE that Europeans—who were using Roman numerals—learned Arabic numerals from Arabs in North Africa. It was much easier to do math with Arabic numerals than with Roman numerals.

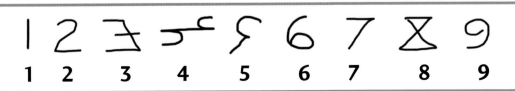

The shape of Arabic numerals developed over time. Shown here are Arabic numerals used in the 10th century CE, along with the Arabic numerals we use today.

Pinhole cameras that took photographs, like the one shown here, were popular in the late 1800s and early 1900s.

A pinhole camera creates a smaller, upside-down image of an object.

Pinhole Camera

In the 11th century CE, Hasan ibn al-Haitham became the first person to clearly describe how to construct a camera. This camera did not capture photographs, but it made possible the invention of photography centuries later.

Al-Haitham discovered that when light reflects off an object and passes through a small hole into a dark space, an upside-down image of the object will appear on a flat white surface. To demonstrate this, he constructed a dark room that had a tiny hole on one side and a white sheet hanging on the opposite side. The light that came through the hole produced an image of what was on the other side of the hole.

Why is this dark room with a tiny hole called a camera? Al-Haitham used the Arabic term *al-Bayt al-Muthlim* (which means "dark room"). This term was translated into Latin as *camera obscura* (*camera* means "room" and *obscura* means "dark"), which led to the English word *camera*. In modern cameras, light passes through a tiny hole into a dark space inside the camera.

Cotton and Wool Mattresses

The English word *mattress* comes from the Arabic word *matrah*, which can mean "mat" or "cushion" or "the place where a cushion is thrown." Some experts believe that Arabs were the first to sleep on mattresses that were like large cushions—they were made of heavy cloth filled with cotton or wool. These soft mattresses were much more comfortable than earlier mattresses, which were sometimes made of leaves or straw covered with animal skin. European soldiers who fought in Arab lands during the Middle Ages took home the idea of sleeping on mattresses filled with cotton or wool.

This photograph from the mid-1930s shows a traditional Arab mattress and cushion.

Crystal Drinking Glasses

The word *crystal* is sometimes used to refer to the high-quality glass from which some wineglasses and chandeliers are made. Designs can be cut into the crystal—which is then called "cut crystal"—to make it sparkle more.

Some experts say that crystal drinking glasses were invented in Italy during the 15th century, but others believe that Arabs were creating crystal glasses long before this. Evidence suggests that in the 9th century CE, the inventor Abbas ibn Firnas discovered a new way to create crystal glass from sand and created the first crystal drinking glasses, which were made of cut crystal. (For other inventions by Abbas ibn Firnas, see page 17.)

A medieval cut-crystal drinking glass, possibly made in Egypt or Syria

ARCHITECTURE

Arabs were famous for constructing large and beautiful buildings such as palaces and mosques. Many of the features that made these buildings beautiful—and well suited to their purpose—were inventions or innovations of Arab architects.

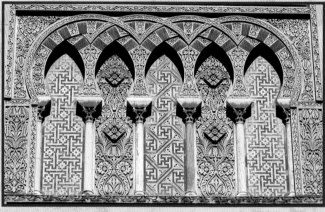

Intersecting arches overlap or cross over one another.

Arches

Arches are semicircular structures often seen in buildings and bridges. The purpose of an arch is to support the weight of the construction materials above it. Ancient Egyptians, Greeks, and Romans all built arches, but Arabs were considered to be masters of the arch because they developed new and creative types of arches.

The horseshoe arch is shaped like a horseshoe— wide in the middle and narrower at the bottom.

The multifoil arch contains several smaller arch shapes.

Round Towers

In the Middle Ages, Europeans fought Arabs in a series of wars known as the Crusades. During the 12th century CE, European soldiers were impressed by the large castles they saw in Arab lands. However, they were not pleased to see that these castles had features that made them difficult to conquer. One of these features was the round tower, which was much stronger than the square towers found in European castles of the time. Round towers were also much more difficult for attackers to climb in attempts to get inside castles. After these soldiers brought news of round towers back to Europe, many European castles were built with round towers.

Round towers at the Aljaferia Palace in Spain

Soldiers dropping stones through machicolations

Machicolations

A parapet is a low wall built along the edge of a roof. On castles, a parapet provided protection for soldiers fighting off an attack. Sometimes a parapet extended out over the wall below it, and had narrow gaps or holes called "machicolations" (pronounced *mah-chi-kuh-lay-shuns*). The machicolations allowed soldiers to fire arrows, drop stones, or pour hot water on the attackers below.

Arabs constructed the very first machicolations in 729 CE, in a castle called *Qasr al-Hayr al-Sharqi* in Syria. European castle builders later copied this architectural feature.

Arrows indicate the location of machicolations at Qasr al-Hayr al-Sharqi in Syria.

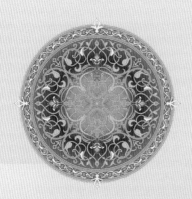

Minarets

One common feature of a mosque is a tall tower called a "minaret." Five times a day, a man known as a muezzin (pronounced *moo-eh-zin*) climbs to the top of the minaret and calls out to Muslims that it is time to pray. While some mosques have four minarets, others have only one or two. Minarets have been built in several different shapes, including slender round towers and thick square towers.

Arabs built the first minaret in 852 CE as part of the Great Mosque of Samarra. (Samarra is a city in Iraq.) Some experts believe the minaret gave Europeans the idea to build churches with tall spires. Spires were first constructed on European churches after soldiers returned from the Crusades.

The minaret at the Great Mosque of Samarra in Iraq is known as the Malwiya (Arabic for "snail shell") because of its spiral shape.

This square minaret is part of a modern mosque in France.

ARCHITECTURE *continued*

Rose Windows

Many large churches have a circular window, often made of stained glass, above the main entrance. This is called a "rose window" because its shape and design make it look like a flower with many petals. (For more information on stained glass, see page 20.)

Early circular windows were openings made to let in light, but they were not covered with glass. Some say that ancient Romans invented circular windows, but the circular openings in their buildings were in the roof, not in the walls. The first large circular window resembling a flower was built by Arabs in 750 CE. It is found in the ruins of the outer wall of the Palace of Khirbat al-Mafjar, located near the city of Jericho (called *Ariha* in Arabic) in modern-day West Bank, which is part of the Palestinian Territories.

The round "rose window" in the ruins of the Palace of Khirbat al-Mafjar

Skyscraper City

The term "skyscraper" was first used in the United States during the 1800s to describe a building that had more than 10 floors, which was considered amazingly high at the time. Some people call New York City a "skyscraper city" because it has so many extremely tall buildings.

Back in the 1500s CE, Arabs built mud-brick "tower houses" in Shibam, Yemen, to protect the people from floods and from attacks by Bedouins. While these buildings had only five to eleven floors, they were unusually tall for the time. Because about 500 of these tower houses were built, some people consider Shibam to have been the very first skyscraper city.

Mud-brick "skyscrapers" in Shibam, Yemen

CONTRIBUTIONS OF ARAB WOMEN

Author's note: History often overlooks the achievements of women. In this book, it was important to me to acknowledge the contributions of Arab women from the past. The achievements of the women on this page are just a small sample of the many ways in which women have played an important and active role in Arab society.

Providing Water and Shelter on the Way to Mecca

Zubayda bint Jafar al-Mansur was the wife of a caliph and the most powerful woman in the Arab empire in the 9th century CE. She wanted to help travelers making the long and difficult journey from Baghdad to Mecca, which involved crossing the hot desert, so she provided money to dig wells and build *khans* all along the route. The wells provided clean drinking water, and the *khans* were like motels, where travelers and their camels were given free food and a place to sleep overnight. The route was later named *Darb Zubayda* (or Zubayda's Way) in her honor. (For more information on Mecca and to learn about the journey to Mecca known as the Hajj, see page 28.)

Funding a School

Fatima al-Fehri lived in Fez, Morocco, during the 9th century CE. When she inherited money from her father, a wealthy businessman, she wanted to use it in a way that would benefit her city. She donated money to build a school that became the University of al-Qarawiyin (see page 15). She was nicknamed *Umm al-Banine*, which means "mother of the boys" (the "boys" were the students).

Making High-Quality Astrolabes

Maerium al-Ijliya al-Astrulabi, who lived in the 10th century CE, became famous as an astrolabe-maker for two reasons: at that time it was an unusual profession for a woman, and she became a master of her craft while still young, before her death at age 23. After learning how to make astrolabes from her father, she worked for Sayf al-Dawla, the ruler of northern Syria. (For more information on astrolabes, see page 17.)

Solving Math Problems

Sutayta al-Mahamali was an expert mathematician in the 10th century CE who was able to find solutions to complicated math problems that other mathematicians had been unable to solve. She belonged to an educated family in Baghdad and had been taught by many scholars, including her father, who was a judge.

Creating the First Women's Shelter

Al-Shaykh Zainab lived in Egypt during the 13th century CE. She worked with the daughter of the sultan (ruler) of Egypt to establish the world's first women's shelter—a safe place to live for women who felt abused and threatened in their own homes. At the shelter, women were provided with counseling, education, and social services.

THE ARAB WORLD TODAY

The Arab world today is a unique combination of ancient traditions and modern innovations. While cultural practices and religion continue to play an important role, Arabs embrace the latest scientific and technological innovations of the 21st century.

Oil

The discovery of oil in Arab countries during the 1930s brought many changes to the Arab world. Selling oil to nations around the globe provided money for building modern highways, houses, office buildings, and other facilities. People from all over the world moved to Arab countries to work in the oil industry, which continues to provide—among other things—fuel for cars and factories worldwide.

Architecture and Engineering

Like their ancestors, Arabs engage in construction projects that are impressive and unique. Perhaps the most unusual is Dubai's Palm Jumeriah, an artificial island that is shaped like a palm tree. In Manama, Bahrain, the very modern Bahrain World Trade Center features two sail-shaped towers linked by three skybridges. Powerful wind turbines located on the skybridges use wind energy to produce some of the electricity needed by the towers.

The Bahrain World Trade Center

Transportation

The days when camels were used to transport goods and people are long gone. In the Arab world today, you can find examples of the latest advances in transportation. For instance, the Dubai Metro in the United Arab Emirates is the world's longest fully automated public transportation network, with trains that run both underground and aboveground. The King Fahd Causeway is a four-lane highway that crosses the Gulf of Bahrain, connecting the island kingdom of Bahrain to Saudi Arabia. At Jeddah International Airport in Saudi Arabia, the Hajj Terminal was built for pilgrims traveling to Mecca and Medina. This terminal's unique roof is designed to look like the tops of many large tents, and it covers more area than any other roof in the world.

The Hajj Terminal at Jeddah International Airport (above), and one of the stations of the Dubai Metro system (below)

Media

Today, the majority of the Arab population is under the age of 30, so it's not surprising that social media such as Twitter and Facebook have become very popular in the Arab world. Arab perspectives on world events—broadcast in Arabic—are now available in countries around the globe through cable news networks such as Al-Jazeera, CNN Arabic, and BBC Arabic.

Tourism

Arabs have a long tradition of making visitors feel welcome. In recent years, cities in Dubai and Bahrain have become popular destinations, especially for tourists seeking luxurious accommodations. The Mall of the Emirates in Dubai offers an indoor ski resort.

People who enjoy history can visit the ancient city of Petra, in Jordan, to view rock-cut architecture dating from the 6th century BCE. They might also visit the beautiful old palaces and fountains in the capital city of Tunisia, called Tunis, which was founded in 698 CE. Tourists enjoy exploring the narrow alleyways of the Casbah (Arabic for "fortress"), in Algiers, the capital city of Algeria.

Ancient buildings carved from rock in Petra, Jordan

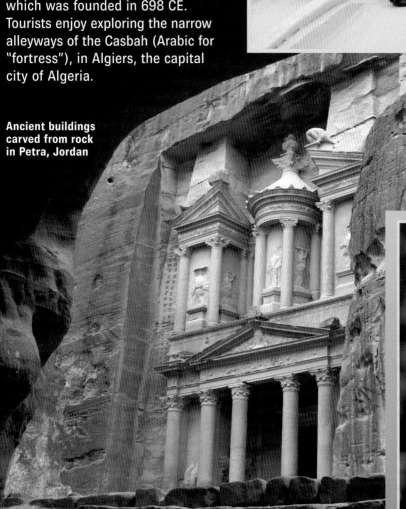

Soccer

Soccer (which many Arabs call "football") is the most popular sport in the Arab world. Teams from Saudi Arabia and Tunisia have played in the FIFA World Cup. The Egyptian soccer team has been ranked as one of the 10 best in the world. One of the most popular soccer players is Zinedine Zidane, a French player of Arab origin. Zidane recently represented Qatar in its successful bid to host the 2022 FIFA World Cup.

Past and Future

While in many ways the Arab world embraces both ancient traditions and modern developments, in some aspects of Arab society there is tension between old and new. This is especially true for issues concerned with politics and the role of women in society. Starting in December 2010, large protests were held in many Arab countries by people supporting political and social change. This wave of protests became known around the world as the "Arab Spring" (because spring represents a new beginning).

As the Arab world finds its way through the 21st century, Arab countries will continue to play an influential role in world politics, and people of Arab heritage around the world will continue to take pride in Arab culture, both past and present.

Tawakkol Karman from Yemen was awarded the Nobel Peace Prize in 2011.

A large protest in Cairo, Egypt

A Note on the Arabic Language

Arabic is the main language for most of the Arab world. Over 300 million people around the world speak Arabic as their first language. It is also spoken by many people who have a different first language.

While Arabic can be written using the English alphabet (as seen in examples of Arabic words throughout this book), it is usually written using the Arabic alphabet. When using the Arabic alphabet, texts are written from right to left across the page.

The Arabic Alphabet

The Arabic alphabet is shown below. (Read the alphabet from right to left.) The letter names are presented using the English alphabet. Each letter name shown is similar to the sound the letter makes.

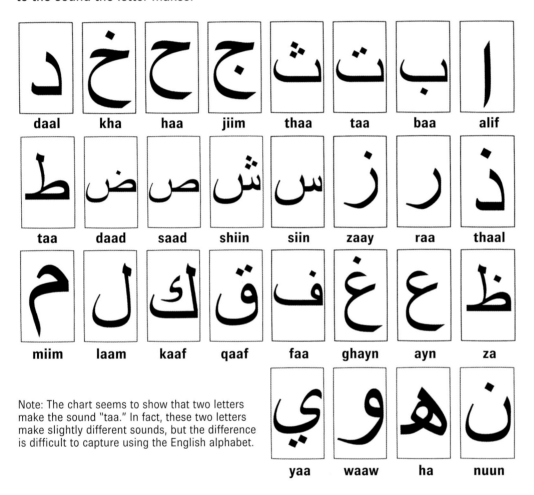

| daal | kha | haa | jiim | thaa | taa | baa | alif |

| taa | daad | saad | shiin | siin | zaay | raa | thaal |

| miim | laam | kaaf | qaaf | faa | ghayn | ayn | za |

| | | | | yaa | waaw | ha | nuun |

Note: The chart seems to show that two letters make the sound "taa." In fact, these two letters make slightly different sounds, but the difference is difficult to capture using the English alphabet.

From Arabic to English

Many words came into the English language from Arabic. Here are a few examples.

English Word	Original Arabic Word	English Word	Original Arabic Word
chemistry	keemiya	lime	lima
cotton	qutn	mascara	muskara
giraffe	zaraffa	mattress	matrah
jar	jarra	safari	safariya
lemon	limun	sofa	suffah

Further Reading

Barber, Nicola. *Everyday Life in the Ancient Arab and Islamic World.* North Mankato, MN: Smart Apple Media, 2006.

Barber, Nicola. *Peoples and Cultures of the Middle East* (World Almanac Library of the Middle East series). Milwaukee, WI: World Almanac Library, 2006.

Barnard, Bryn. *The Genius of Islam: How Muslims Made the Modern World.* New York: Alfred A. Knopf, 2011.

Blanchard, Anne. *Arab Science and Invention in the Golden Age.* Brooklyn, NY: Enchanted Lion Books, 2009.

Hinds, Kathryn. *The City* (Life in the Medieval Muslim World series). Tarrytown, NY: Marshall Cavendish, 2008.

Steele, Philip. *The Middle East* (Kingfisher Knowledge series). London: Kingfisher Publications, 2009.

Stone, Caroline. *Islam* (DK Eyewitness Books series). New York: Dorling Kindersley, 2005.

Selected Sources

Hattstein, Markus, and Peter Delius, eds. *Islam: Art and Architecture.* Cologne: Konemann, 2000.

Hoyland, Robert G. *Arabia and the Arabs: From the Bronze Age to the Coming of Islam.* London: Routledge, 2001.

Khalili, Jim al-. *The House of Wisdom: How Arabic Science Saved Ancient Knowledge and Gave Us the Renaissance.* New York: Penguin, 2011.

Khalili, Jim al-. *Pathfinders: The Golden Age of Arabic Science.* London: Allen Lane, 2010.

Lyons, Jonathan. *House of Wisdom: How the Arabs Transformed Western Civilization.* New York: Bloomsbury Press, 2009.

Morgan, Michael Hamilton. *Lost History: The Enduring Legacy of Muslim Scientists, Thinkers, and Artists.* Washington, DC: National Geographic, 2007.

Credits

Index

SAIMA SHAKIL HUSSAIN grew up in Dammam, Saudi Arabia. Soon after graduating from the University of Toronto with an Honours B.A. in English and History, she returned to that university and completed an M.A. at the Munk School of Global Affairs.

Saima was a university admissions counselor for five years before traveling overseas, where she worked as a journalist in Pakistan. Her travels also include several trips back to Saudi Arabia, as well as visits to Dubai. Along with travel, her interests include reading about the history of various countries and trying new foods.

Saima lives in Mississauga, Ontario. This is her first book.

Also in Annick's acclaimed We Thought of It series:

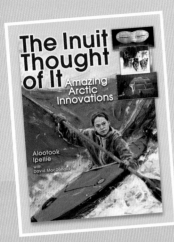

★ Children's "Non-Fiction Top 10" List,
  Ontario Library Association
★ 2008 Skipping Stones Honor Award

"[An] informative and easy to read book ...
attractive and useful."
—*Children's Book News*

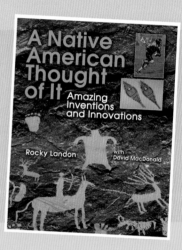

★ Best Books for Kids & Teens 2009, Canadian
  Children's Book Centre
★ "The Year's Best" List, *Resource Links*

"Deserves a permanent spot on any
reader's bookshelf."
—*ForeWord Reviews*

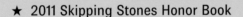

★ "Best Bets" List, Ontario Library Association
★ 2010 Best Books, Canadian Children's Book Centre

"A well-focused introduction to the history of
technological innovation in China."
—*Booklist Online*

★ 2011 Skipping Stones Honor Book

"This book is a wealth of information for anyone
studying about African countries and their cultures."
—*CM Magazine*

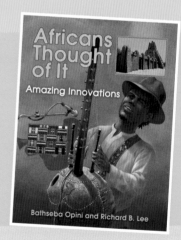

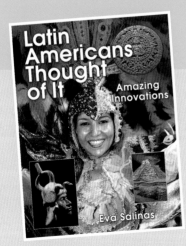

"I like the series and love that it brings our attention to technological
advancements that developed in other places and times outside of North America.
Good introductions that could lead into deeper discussions and research."
—*Doucette Library of Teaching Resources*

Also available in Spanish, as *Lo Inventaron los Latinoamericanos:
Innovaciones asombrosas*

Go to www.annickpress.com to view book trailers for these and other exciting titles.